The material was previously published in the book *Scrumptious Toppers for Tots & Toddlers* (ISBN 978-1-56158-998-2) First published in this format 2012

The Taunton Press
Inspiration for hands-on living®

The Taunton Press, Inc.,
63 South Main Street,
PO Box 5506,
Newtown, CT 06470-5506
e-mail: tp@taunton.com

Interior Design: Deborah Kerner
Photographer: James Roderick

Printed in the United States of America
10 9 8 7 6 5 4 3 2 1

Table of Contents

Birthday Cupcake Cap

This sugar-coated hat is so sweet you'll want to eat it up! With French Knots, you create festive sprinkles, and the candle in the middle has a little glittery flame to help celebrate the special day.

Sizing

Newborn to 1 year (14-in. circumference)

Yarn

Light Weight (CYCA 3), Smooth Yarn, approx. 60 yd. Pink or Blue, 3 yd. Red, 5 yd. White

Bulky Weight (CYCA 5), Boucle Yarn, approx. 2 yd. Green

Light Weight (CYCA 3), Eyelash Yarn, approx. 3 yd. Yellow

Shown in

S.R. Kertzer Super 10 Cotton #3446 Cotton Candy or #3841 Caribbean

S.R. Kertzer Super 10 Cotton #3997 Scarlet

S.R. Kertzer Super 10 Cotton White

Lion Brand Homespun #790-389 Spring Green

Stylecraft Icicle #1143 Sunlight

Materials

16-in. U.S. size 4 circular needle

Four U.S. size 4 double-pointed needles

Stitch marker

Tapestry needle

GAUGE

22 sts = 4 in. with Light Weight Smooth Yarn

SEED STITCH

Rnd 1: *K1, P1; rep from * to end of rnd.

All other rnds: K the P sts and P the K sts.

Directions

HAT BASE

With circ needles and Pink/Blue, CO 72 sts. Place a st marker on right needle and, beginning Rnd 1, join CO sts together making sure that sts do not become twisted on needle.

Rnd 1: P.

Work Seed st for 3 in.

Cut Pink/Blue and attach Green.

K1 rnd. P1 rnd.

Cut Green and attach Yellow eyelash.

CROWN

With Yellow eyelash, work Seed st on all rnds for
approx 2 in.

DECREASE ROUNDS

Dec Rnd 1: *K7, K2tog; rep from * to end
of rnd.

Dec Rnd 2: *K6, K2tog; rep from * to end
of rnd.

Dec Rnd 3: *K5, K2tog; rep from * to end
of rnd.

Continue in established pattern, knitting one less
st between dec and changing to dpns when
necessary. Cut yarn, leaving a 6-in. tail. Using
a tapestry needle, thread the tail through
the rem sts on the needles. Pull the yarn,
gathering sts tightly together, then secure the
tail on the WS of work.

BIRTHDAY CANDLE

With 2 dpns and White, CO 7 sts.

Work I-Cord (see p.134) for 14 rnds.

Cut White, attach Yellow eyelash, and work 3
rnds.

Cut Yellow eyelash and, using a tapestry needle,
thread the Yellow eyelash and White tails
through the rem sts on the needle and pass
all tails through the inside of the I-Cord.

Using those tails, attach the candle securely to
the tip of the hat for a candle that will never
burn out! Make French Knots with Red to
create sprinkles on the top of your cupcake.

WELT

Thread a tapestry needle with White, pinch the
hat at the Green pure rnd, and create a Welt
by sewing together the top and bottom pieces
using even running stitches.

FINISHING

Weave in all loose ends. Now it's birthday time!

Baby Beastie Beanie

With a little smirk and sparkling ear tips, this charming hat can be your littlest one's best animal pal. It is so easy and quick to knit that you'll soon have a bunch of beasties at your fingertips!

Sizing

Newborn to 2 years (14-in. circumference)

Yarn

Light Weight (CYCA 3), Smooth Yarn,
approx. 50 yd. Cream; 20 yd. Pink or
Blue; 2 yd. Green,
Light Weight (CYCA 3), Eyelash Yarn,
approx. 3 yd. White

Shown in

S.R. Kertzer Super 10 Cotton Cream
S.R. Kertzer. Super 10 Cotton #3446 Cotton
Candy or #3841 Caribbean
S.R. Kertzer Super 10 Cotton #3722 Celery
Stylecraft Icicle #1141 Polar

Materials

16-in. U.S. size 4 circular needle
One pair U.S. size 4 straight needles
Stitch marker
Tapestry needle

GAUGE

22 sts = 4 in. with Light Weight Smooth Yarn

Directions

HAT BASE

With circ needles and Cream,
CO 70 sts. Place a st marker on right needle
and, beginning Rnd 1, join CO sts together
making sure that sts do not become twisted
on needle.

Rnd 1: P.
Rnds 2–26: K.

BEASTIE'S EARS

You will divide the work in half and work back
and forth on straight needles—not in the
round—for the remainder of the hat.

Row 1 (RS): K35.
Row 2 (WS): P.
Row 3: K1, sl 1, K1, psso. Work to the last 3
sts. K2tog, K1.
Rep Rows 2 and 3 until 23 sts rem. P1 row.
Cut Cream and attach Pink/Blue. Continue
dec until 7 sts rem on needle. Attach White
Eyelash and K only (Garter st) for 1 in. Cut
all yarn, leaving a 6-in. tail. Thread tapestry
needle and pass it through the rem sts on the
needle. Secure to WS of work.

Attach Cream where the work was divided for first ear and create the second ear following the same directions.

FINISHING

With Cream, thread a tapestry needle with tails and sew the Beastie's head closed, using the photo on the facing page as a reference. The base of this seam will be where the nose is added. Weave in all loose ends.

BEASTIE NOSE

With Pink/Blue and straight needles, CO 1 st. K1f&b 3 times, K1, creating 7 sts from 1 st. Work 5 rows in Garter st.

Dec Row: Sl 1, K1, psso. Work to the last 2 sts and K2tog. Cut the yarn, leaving a 4-in. tail. Thread a tapestry needle and pass it through the rem sts on the needle. Tie CO and BO tails together to form a ball. Attach this to the Beastie at the base of the Cream seam. With Pink/Blue, make 2 French Knots for the eyes. Using the photograph at left as a reference, embroider Green circles around the eyes. With Pink/Blue, embroider your own delightful smirk of a smile.

FINAL TOUCH

Using White Eyelash, make a small French Knot in the middle of the Beastie's nose for an added touch of fun.

Greenie Beanie

This tiny beanie with flowers on top is perfect for your tiny one! It is so easy to create that you'll want to knit one in every color of the rainbow.

Sizing

Newborn (13-in. circumference) to 2 years (16-in. circumference)

Figures for larger size are given below in parentheses. Where only one set of figures appears, the directions apply to both sizes.

Yarn

Light Weight (CYCA 3), Smooth Yarn, approx. 60 (70) yd. Green; 10 yd. Light Yellow; 10 yd. Blue; 10 yd. Bright Yellow

Shown in

S.R. Kertzer Super 10 Cotton #3722 Celery
S.R. Kertzer Super 10 Cotton #3525 Cornsilk
S.R. Kertzer Super 10 Cotton #3841 Caribbean
S.R. Kertzer Super 10 Cotton #3533 Daffodil

Materials

16-in. U.S. size 4 circular needle
Four U.S. size 4 double-pointed needles
Stitch marker
Tapestry needle

GAUGE

22 sts = 4 in.

SEED STITCH

Rnd 1: *K1, P1; rep from * to end of rnd.
All other rnds: K the P sts and P the K sts.

Directions

HAT BASE

With circ needles and Green, CO 60 (70) sts. Place a st marker on right needle and, beginning Rnd 1, join CO sts together making sure that sts do not become twisted on needle.

Rnd 1: P.

Work Seed st for 3 1/2 (4) in.

Drop Green and attach Light Yellow. K1 rnd, P1 rnd.

Cut Light Yellow and pick up Green. Work Seed st an additional 2 in.

Length of beanie from base should be 6 (7) in. Cut yarn, leaving an 8-in. tail. Using a tapestry needle, thread the tail through all the sts on the needle. Pull the yarn, gathering the sts tightly together, then secure the tail on the WS of the beanie.

STEMS

With Blue, CO 6 sts and work I-Cord for 20 rows. Make 2 I-Cords.

LEAVES

With Green and 2 dpns, CO 4 sts. K1 row. At beg of each following row, K1, Kf&b, K across until you have 8 sts. K1 row. At beg of each following row, K2tog, K across until 4 sts rem. BO all sts.
Make 2 leaves.

FLOWERS

With Bright Yellow and 2 dpns, CO 14 sts. Kf&b into each st. BO pw. Curl into a flower.
Make 2 flowers.

FINISHING

Sew the stems onto the top of the hat. Attach a leaf to each one, then attach the flower to the top. Weave in all loose ends.

Fancy Scrumptious Beanie

Worked in Seed stitch, this pastel jewel of a beanie is a sweet choice for baby's homecoming. Finger toppers add just the right amount of playfulness.

Sizing

Newborn (12-in. circumference) to 6 months (14-in. circumference)

Figures for larger size are given below in parentheses. Where only one set of figures appears, the directions apply to both sizes.

Yarn

Light Weight (CYCA 3), Smooth Yarn, approx. 30 (35) yd. White; 40 (55) yd. Multi

Shown in

S.R. Kertzer Super 10 Cotton White

S.R. Kertzer Super 10 Cotton Multi #2015 Early Spring

Materials

16-in. U.S. size 4 circular needle

Four U.S. size 4 double-pointed needles

Stitch marker

Tapestry needle

GAUGE

22 sts = 4 in.

SEED STITCH

Rnd 1: *K1, P1; rep from * to end of rnd.

All other rnds: K the P sts and P the K sts.

Directions

HAT BASE

With circ needles and White, CO 81 (99) sts. Place a st marker on right needle and, beginning Rnd 1, join CO sts together making sure that sts do not become twisted on needle.

Note: Always keep unworked yarn on the WS of your work and sl sts pw.

Rnd 1: P.

FIRST TIER

Rnd 1: Attach Multi. *K1 with White, K1 with Multi; rep from * to end of rnd.

Rnd 2: Drop White. *Sl 1 wyib (White st), P1 with Multi; rep from * to end of rnd.

Rnd 3: *K1 with White, P1 with Multi; rep from * to end of rnd.

Rnds 4 & 5: Rep Rnd 3.

Rnd 6: K with White.

Rnd 7: P with White.

SECOND TIER

Rnd 1: *K1 with Multi, K1 with White; rep from * to end of rnd.

Rnd 2: Drop Multi. *Sl 1 wyib (Multi st), P1 with White; rep from * to end of rnd.

Rnd 3: *P1 with Multi, K1 with White; rep from * to end of rnd.

Rnds 4 & 5: Rep Rnd 3.

Rnd 6: K with White.

Rnd 7: P with White.

THIRD TIER

Rep First Tier rnds.

Cut White and with Multi, K1 rnd, then work Seed st for 3 (4) in.

DECREASE ROUNDS

Dec Rnd 1: *K7, K2tog; rep from * to end of rnd.

Dec Rnd 2: *K6, K2tog; rep from * to end of rnd.

Continue in established dec pattern, knitting 1 less st between dec and switching to dpns when necessary until 5 sts rem.

FINGER TOPPERS

Using the Cable Cast-On, CO 5 sts. BO those 5 sts. Rep for entire rnd. Cut yarn, leaving a 6-in. tail. Thread tapestry needle and pass the yarn through the rem sts on needle. Secure to WS of work.

CREATE WELT

Thread a tapestry needle with White, pinch the hat at the last White pure rnd, and create a Welt by sewing together the top and bottom pieces using even running stitches. Pull slightly on White yarn to create a pucker effect that makes the crown flow over the top tier. Weave in all loose ends.

Pretty-in-Pink Cap

This delectable hat takes the cake! Giant yellow bobbles and swirling minty-green "icing" make it absolutely irresistible!

Sizing

3 months to 1 year (15-in. circumference)

Yarn

Light Weight (CYCA 3), Smooth Yarn, approx. 40 yd. Yellow, 4 yd. Pink

Medium Weight (CYCA 4), Ribbon Yarn, approx. 80 yd. Pink

Bulky Weight (CYCA 5), Boucle Yarn, approx. 30 yd. Green

Shown in

S.R. Kertzer Super 10 Cotton #3553 Canary

S.R. Kertzer Super 10 Cotton #3454 Bubblegum

Trendsetter Yarns Skye #1889 Carnation

Lion Brand Yarn Homespun® #790-389 Spring Green

Materials

16-in. U.S. size 4 circular needle

Four U.S. size 4 double-pointed needles

Stitch marker

Tapestry needle

Pom Pom maker (1½ in.)

GAUGE

22 sts = 4 in. with Light Weight Smooth Yarn

Directions

HAT BASE

With circ needles and Green, CO 80 sts. Place a st marker on right needle and, beginning Rnd 1, join CO sts together making sure that sts do not become twisted on needle.

Rnd 1: P.

Rnd 2: P.

Rnds 3–6: K.

Cut Green and attach Pink Ribbon.

K1 rnd. Attach Yellow.

BOBBLE ROUND 1

*MB (see p. 21 for Bobble instructions) with Yellow. Drop Yellow and K4 with Pink Ribbon; rep from * to end of rnd.

Drop Yellow and K3 rnds with Pink Ribbon.

BOBBLE ROUND 2

K2 with Pink Ribbon. *MB with Yellow. Drop
Yellow and K4 with Pink Ribbon; rep from *.
End K3 with Pink Ribbon.

Drop Yellow and K3 rnds with Pink Ribbon.

Rep Bobble Round 1.

Drop Yellow and K3 rnds with Pink Ribbon.

BOBBLE INSTRUCTIONS

With desired color yarn, K1, P1, K1 in the next
st to make 3 sts from 1. Turn and K3, then lift
the second and third sts over the first st on the
right needle.

STRIPES

*Drop Pink Ribbon and K1 rnd with Yellow.
P1 rnd. Drop Yellow and K3 rnds with Pink
Ribbon. Rep from * 4 times. After last rnd, cut
Yellow and attach Green.

CROWN DECREASES

Dec Rnd 1: *K8, K2tog; rep from * to end
of rnd.

Dec Rnd 2: *K7, K2tog; rep from * to end
of rnd.

Continue in established pattern, changing to
dpns when necessary, until approx 4–6 sts
rem. Cut the yarn, leaving a 6-in. tail. Using
a tapestry needle, thread the tail through
the rem sts on the needles. Pull the yarn,
gathering sts tightly together, then secure the
tail on the WS of the work.

WELT

Thread a tapestry needle with Pink Smooth
Yarn, pinch the hat together between the top
of the second Yellow stripe and the bottom
of the fourth Yellow stripe, and create a welt
by sewing the pieces together with evenly
spaced running stitches. Secure ends on WS
of hat.

POM POM

Using Pink Ribbon and Yellow, make Pom Pom
(see p. 31) and attach to top of hat.

FINISHING

Weave in all loose ends.

Peppermint Candy Cap

Giant Pom Poms and a swirly-ridged crown make this cap perfect for your own little peppermint sweetie.

Sizing

Newborn (14-in. circumference) to 2 years (16-in. circumference)

Figures for larger size are given below in parentheses. Where only one set of figures appears, the directions apply to both sizes.

Yarn

Light Weight (CYCA 3), Smooth Yarn, approx. 60 (70) yd. Light Pink; 25 yd. Green; 10 yd. Red; 40 yd. Dark Pink

Light Weight (CYCA 3), Eyelash Yarn, approx. 5 yd. Pink

Shown in

S.R. Kertzer Super 10 Cotton #3443 Shell Pink
S.R. Kertzer Super 10 Cotton #3722 Celery
S.R. Kertzer Super 10 Cotton #3997 Scarlet
S.R. Kertzer Super 10 Cotton #3475 Geranium
Stylecraft Icicle #1140 Crystal

Materials

16-in. U.S. size 4 circular needle
Four U.S. size 4 double-pointed needles
Stitch marker
Tapestry needle
Pom Pom maker ($1\frac{1}{2}$ in.)

GAUGE

22 sts = 4 in. with Light Weight Smooth Yarn

Directions

HAT BASE

With circ needles and Red, CO 72 (80) sts. Place a st marker on right needle and, beginning Rnd 1, join CO sts together making sure that sts do not become twisted on needle.

Rnd 1: P.

Rnd 2: Cut Red. K entire rnd with Light Pink.

Rnd 3: P with Light Pink.

Rnd 4: Drop Light Pink. Attach Dark Pink and K entire rnd.

Rnd 5: P with Dark Pink.

Rep Rnds 2–5 until you have 4 ridges of Light
Pink and 3 ridges of Dark Pink. Cut Dark Pink,
attach Red, and K entire rnd. P next rnd. Cut
Red and pick up Light Pink.

INCREASE ROUND

With Light Pink *K1, K1f&b; rep from * to end of
rnd—108 (120) sts.

K with Light Pink for a total of 12 rnds.

Drop Light Pink. Attach Green. *K1 rnd. P1 rnd.
Drop Green, pick up Light Pink, and K4 rnds;
drop Light Pink, pick up Green, and rep from *
until you have a total of 4 Green ridges.

SWIRL TOP

Cut Light Pink and Green. Attach Dark Pink
and start dec rnds, changing to dpns when
necessary.

Dec Rnd 1: *K7 (8), K2tog; rep from * to end
of rnd.

Dec Rnd 2: *K6 (7), K2tog; rep from * to end
of rnd. Continue in established pattern,
knitting 1 less st between decs. When 4–6
sts rem, cut the yarn, leaving a 6-in. tail.
Thread a tapestry needle and pass it through
the remaining sts left on the needle. Bring the
tail to the WS of the work.

FINISHING

Weave in all loose ends.

Thread a tapestry needle with Dark Pink, pinch
the hat at the first Green pure rnd, and create
a Welt by sewing together the top and bottom
pieces using even running stitches.

Using Light Pink and Pink Eyelash, make three
Pom Poms (see p. 31) and attach them
securely to the top of the hat.

Wee Wild One

A big smile lies under that big sparkling nose. Add some wild hair and a pair of glittery ears, and you have a friendly face for your little wild one.

Sizing

6 months to 2 years (16-in. circumference)

Yarn

Light Weight (CYCA 3), Smooth Yarn,
approx. 60 yd. Pink or Blue;
15 yd. Purple; 15 yd. Green;
2 yd. Dark Pink, 1 yd. Black
Light Weight (CYCA 3), Eyelash Yarn,
approx. 20 yd. Pink or Blue

Shown in

S.R. Kertzer Super 10 Cotton #3446 Cotton
Candy or #3841 Caribbean
S.R. Kertzer Super 10 Cotton #3936 Wisteria
S.R. Kertzer Super 10 Cotton #3722 Celery
S.R. Kertzer Super 10 Cotton #3454 Bubblegum
S.R. Kertzer Super 10 Cotton Black
Stylecraft Icicle #1143 Artic (blue) or
#1140 Crystal (pink)

Materials

16-in. U.S. size 4 circular needle
One pair U.S. size 4 straight needles
Stitch marker
Tapestry needle
Pom Pom maker (1 in.)

GAUGE

22 sts = 4 in. with Light Weight Smooth Yarn

Directions

HAT BASE

With circ needle and Pink/Blue, CO 70. Place a
st marker on right needle and, beginning Rnd
1, join CO sts together making sure that sts
do not become twisted on needle.

Rnd 1: P.

Rnds 2–25: K.

HAIR

Attach Green and Purple. *MB (see p. 21 for
Bobble instructions) with Purple. K1 with
Pink/Blue. Using the Cable Cast-On, pick up

Rep Rows 2 and 3 until 23 sts remain. P1 row. Cut Pink/Blue and attach Pink/Blue Eyelash. K every row (Garter st) for the remainder of the ear, continuing decs as established until 4–5 sts rem on the needle. Cut the yarn, leaving a 6-in. tail. Thread the tapestry needle and pass it through the rem sts. Secure to WS of work.

Attach Pink/Blue where the work was divided for the first ear and create the second ear following the same directions.

FINISHING

With Pink/Blue, thread the tapestry needle with tails and sew the Wild One's head closed. Weave in all loose ends.

SPARKLY NOSE

Using Pink/Blue and matching Icicle, make a large Pom Pom (see p. 31) and attach it to the front of hat below the seam and hair.

Embroider eyes and a big grin onto the face of the hat using Black and Dark Pink. See the photograph on the facing page for visual reference.

Green and create one "hair" as follows: CO 8 sts. BO those 8 sts. K1 with Pink/Blue; rep from * for entire rnd. Now our wee one has some wild hair!

EARS

For the ears, divide the work in half and work back and forth on straight needles—not in the round—for the remainder of the hat.

Row 1 (RS): K35.

Row 2: P.

Row 3: K1, sl 1, K1, psso. Work until 3 sts rem, K2tog, K1.

Abbreviations

approx	approximately
beg	beginning
BO	bind off
circ	circular
CO	cast on
cont	continue
dec	decrease/decreases/decreasing
dpn(s)	double-pointed needle(s)
inc	increase/increases/increasing
K	knit
K1f&b	knit in the front and in the back of the same stitch
K2tog	knit 2 stitches together
kw	knitwise
M1	make 1 stitch
MB	make bobble
P	Purl
psso	pass slipped stitch over
pw	purlwise
rem	remaining
rep	repeat
rnd	round
RS	right side
skp	slip 1, knit 1, pass slipped stitch over knit 1
sl 1	slip 1 stitch
st(s)	stitch(es)
St st	stockinette stitch
tog	together
WS	wrong side
wyib	with yarn in back of work
yd	yard/yards
YO	yarn over

Standard Yarn Weights

NUMBERED BALL	DESCRIPTION	STS/4 IN.	NEEDLE SIZE
1 SUPER FINE	Sock, baby, fingering	27–32	2.25–3.25 mm (U.S. 1–3)
2 FINE	Sport, baby	23–26	3.25–3.75 mm (U.S. 3–5)
3 LIGHT	DK, light worsted	21–24	3.75–4.5 mm (U.S. 5–7)
4 MEDIUM	Worsted, afghan, Aran	16–20	4.5–5.5 mm (U.S. 7–9)
5 BULKY	Chunky, craft, rug	12–15	5.5–8.0 mm (U.S. 9–11)
6 SUPER BULKY	Bulky, roving	6–11	8 mm and larger (U.S. 11 and larger)

HOW TO MAKE POM POMS

1. Cut out two circles of cardboard (approx. 2.5 inches diameter) and cut a 3/4-inch circle out of the middle of each circle to make two rings.

2. Hold both cardboard rings together and wrap the yarn of your choice around the two rings until the cardboard is covered. The more yarn you wrap, the fuller the pom pom will be.

3. Carefully insert the blade of your scissors into the outer edge of the yarn-wrapped cardboard so that it sits between the two cardboard rings. Hold the center of the ring with your thumb and forefinger and carefully cut all the way around the outside edge.

4. Once the wrapped yarn has been cut, slide a length of yarn between the cardboard rings and tie it around the center of the cut threads. Ease the cardboard rings off the yarn, and tie again to make a tight knot, leaving a long tail. Fluff the pom pom and trim any untidy ends.

Look for these other THREADS Selects booklets at www.taunton.com and wherever crafts are sold.

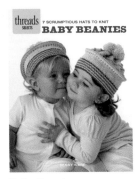

Baby Beanies
Debby Ware

EAN: 9781621137634
8 ½ x 10 ⅞, 32 pages
Product# 078001
$9.95 U.S., $11.95 Can.

Fair Isle Flower Garden
Kathleen Taylor

EAN: 9781621137702
8 ½ x 10 ⅞, 32 pages
Product# 078008
$9.95 U.S., $11.95 Can.

Fair Isle Hats, Scarves, Mittens & Gloves
Kathleen Taylor

EAN: 9781621137719
8 ½ x 10 ⅞, 32 pages
Product# 078009
$9.95 U.S., $11.95 Can.

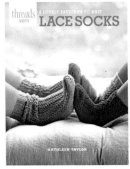

Lace Socks
Kathleen Taylor

EAN: 9781621137894
8 ½ x 10 ⅞, 32 pages
Product# 078012
$9.95 U.S., $11.95 Can.

Colorwork Socks
Kathleen Taylor

EAN: 9781621137740
8 ½ x 10 ⅞, 32 pages
Product# 078011
$9.95 U.S., $11.95 Can.

DIY Bride Cakes & Sweets
Khris Cochran

EAN: 9781621137665
8 ½ x 10 ⅞, 32 pages
Product# 078004
$9.95 U.S., $11.95 Can.

DIY Bride Beautiful Bouquets
Khris Cochran

EAN: 9781621137672
8 ½ x 10 ⅞, 32 pages
Product# 078005
$9.95 U.S., $11.95 Can.

Bead Necklaces
Susan Beal

EAN: 9781621137641
8 ½ x 10 ⅞, 32 pages
Product# 078002
$9.95 U.S., $11.95 Can.

Drop Earrings
Susan Beal

EAN: 9781621137658
8 ½ x 10 ⅞, 32 pages
Product# 078003
$9.95 U.S., $11.95 Can.

Crochet Prayer Shawls
Janet Severi Bristow &
Victoria A. Cole-Galo

EAN: 9781621137689
8 ½ x 10 ⅞, 32 pages
Product# 078006
$9.95 U.S., $11.95 Can.

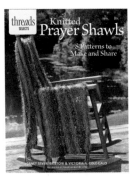

Knitted Prayer Shawls
Janet Severi Bristow &
Victoria A. Cole-Galo

EAN: 9781621137696
8 ½ x 10 ⅞, 32 pages
Product# 078007
$9.95 U.S., $11.95 Can.

Shawlettes
Jean Moss

EAN: 9781621137726
8 ½ x 10 ⅞, 32 pages
Product# 078010
$9.95 U.S., $11.95 Can.

In the Beginning

In the beginning, God created the heaven and the earth.

He said "Let there be light," and made the day and the night.

On the second day, God made the sky and the clouds.

On the third day, God made dry land and seas and grass and trees.

On the fourth day, God made the sun, the moon, and all the stars.

On the fifth day, God made fish and birds.

On the sixth day, God made all the animals.

Then He made a man in His own image. He called him Adam.

On the seventh day, He rested.

The
Bible Story
Coloring Book

Written by
Veda Boyd Jones

Illustrated by
Kathy Arbuckle

A Barbour Book

The Garden of Eden

God built a special garden for Adam to live in. It looked like a beautiful park with fields and woods and rivers. Fruits and vegetables grew there for Adam to eat.

God brought all the animals to Adam and let him name them.

God knew Adam was lonely. So, He put Adam in a deep sleep and took a rib from his side and created woman.

Adam's wife was called Eve.

Together they lived in the beautiful garden, eating the fruit of the trees, drinking from the rivers, and playing with the animals.

Life was wonderful.

The Temptation

God told Adam and Eve they could eat from any tree in the garden except The Tree of the Knowledge of Good and Evil. If they ate the fruit of this tree, they would die.

A snake who lived in the garden told Eve that if she ate the forbidden fruit, she would be as wise as God.

Eve ate the fruit and gave some to Adam. He ate it, too.

God was angry that they had not followed His rule. Now they would die instead of living forever. He sent them from the Garden of Eden into the world.

Noah and the Ark

God looked on the world that was full of wicked people and was angry. He decided to destroy the world and start over.

Of all the people, God found only one man who tried to please Him. He decided to save Noah and his family.

He told Noah to build a big boat, called an ark, and fill it with two of every creature, big and small.

Noah built the ark and filled it with animals. His wife and his sons and their wives climbed on board.

God caused the rain to come. It rained for forty days and forty nights.

The Rainbow

Rain poured down, flooding the land. Houses, treetops, and mountains disappeared. But Noah's ark floated safely on the water.

When the rain stopped and the waters went down, Noah's ark rested on top of a mountain. More than two months passed before God told Noah the land was dry enough for man and animal to live on it again.

Noah built an altar and thanked God for the safe journey.

God was pleased and told Noah he would never again destroy the earth with a giant flood. He placed a rainbow in the sky as His promise.

The Tower of Babel

The land filled with people again. They all lived in the same area. One day they decided to build a great tower that would reach to the heavens.

God did not want the tower built. He wanted the people to live all over the earth, not in one place.

One night while they slept, God changed the speech of the people. When they awoke, they spoke different languages. Since the workmen couldn't understand each other, they couldn't finish the tower.

Those who spoke the same language lived in tribes, and the tribes moved all over the world.

The Story of Abraham

Abram was an old man when God told him to pack his belongings and take his family to a land called Canaan.

Abram obeyed God. His family, their servants and flocks moved to Canaan. They lived in tents in this new land.

God was pleased with Abram. God changed his name to Abraham and promised him he would be the father of a great nation.

"How can that be?" Abraham asked. "I have no children, and I am old."

God promised Abraham that he and his wife Sarah would have a child and his name would be Isaac.

Lot's Wife Turns
to Salt

Two strange men went to the wicked city of Sodom. Lot, a good man, was by the gate and welcomed the two men. He asked them to spend the night in his house, since they wouldn't be safe in the streets.

The men were angels sent by God to destroy Sodom and the nearby city of Gomorrah.

The next morning, the angels rushed Lot, his wife and two daughters out of the city.

"Run! Do not look back," one angel ordered.

Lot's wife looked back at the burning city and was instantly turned into a pillar of salt.

Jacob's Ladder

While traveling alone from his father's home to his uncle's house, Jacob looked for a place to sleep. He found a flat stone and used it for a pillow.

He fell asleep and dreamed. He saw a huge ladder with angels climbing up and down on it. At the top was God Himself.

God told Jacob, just as He had told his grandfather Abraham and his father Isaac, that his family would rule that land. God said he would protect Jacob and help him in all he did.

Jacob promised God one-tenth of everything he received in life, which pleased God.

Joseph is Sold as a Slave

Jacob, also known as Israel, had twelve sons. Joseph was his favorite. Israel loved him so much, he gave Joseph a coat of many colors. This made Joseph's brothers hate him.

God gave Joseph the gift of understanding dreams. This made his brothers hate him even more.

Israel sent Joseph to the pastures to check on his brothers and their flocks. The brothers saw their chance to kill Joseph but instead decided to throw him into a pit.

The brothers told their father that Joseph had been killed by a wild animal.

Joseph and Dreams

Joseph was first sold as a slave, then thrown into prison, where he told prisoners what their dreams meant. Later the Egyptian king sent for Joseph and asked him to interpret his dreams.

God gave Joseph the power to explain the dream of seven fat cows and seven lean cows: a seven-year time of good crops would be followed by seven years of no crops. People would starve. Joseph told the king to appoint a wise man to save food during the good time so the people would have food during the bad time.

The king gave Joseph that job.

Joseph and His Brothers

Joseph's ten brothers came to Egypt to buy food. They spoke with Joseph, who was governor of Egypt, but they didn't know who he was. Joseph knew them, but pretended he didn't. He needed to make sure they had changed their ways and weren't evil. He asked them to bring Benjamin, now his father's favorite son, to Egypt.

When they did this, and proved they would not harm Benjamin, Joseph told them who he was. He forgave them for selling him and told them it was God's will.

Joseph's brothers and his father, now called Israel, moved to Egypt.

A Princess Finds a Baby

Joseph and his brothers died in Egypt, but their family—the people of Israel—grew bigger and bigger. A new king was afraid the Israelites would grow powerful and turn against him. He made them slaves.

He passed a law that all Israelite baby boys should be killed.

To save her baby, one Israelite mother made a basket for her three-month-old baby and floated him on the river where the king's daughter found him.

The princess took the baby and named him Moses. She raised him as her own, but she told him he was an Israelite.

Moses and the Burning Bush

One day Moses was caring for his flock when he saw a burning bush. Although it was on fire, it didn't burn up, as wood does.

God spoke to Moses from the bush and told him to go to Egypt and ask the king to set the Israelites free. He gave Moses power to do certain miracles to prove he was speaking God's Word.

Since Moses' brother Aaron was a better speaker, he also was given these powers.

The brothers went to the king and said "The Lord has said, 'Let My people go.'"

The king laughed and said, "No."

The Plagues and Passover

The king wouldn't let the Israelites leave, so God sent plagues to Egypt. He sent frogs, lice, flies, animal diseases, sores, hail and fire, locusts, and darkness. Still the king wouldn't let the Israelites leave.

God told Moses there would be one more tragedy. In the night, God would pass through Egypt and kill the oldest son in every house.

Each Israelite family killed a lamb and marked the door with its blood. When God saw the blood, He passed over that house and didn't kill the oldest son who lived there.

The next day the king let God's people go.

Parting of the Red Sea

The Israelites followed God's large column-like cloud out of Egypt. At night the cloud glowed so they could see the way. When it stopped, they stopped.

The king heard that the Israelites were near the Red Sea. He took an army to capture them and make them slaves again.

God told Moses to hold his rod over the sea. A strong wind blew the water back, leaving a dry seabed that the Israelites walked across.

The Egyptians followed. God had Moses hold his rod up again, and the water rushed back, drowning the Egyptians and saving the Israelites.

Manna from Heaven

As they walked to Canaan, the Israelites complained to Moses because there was little food in the dry desert. What could they eat? Would they starve?

God heard the cries of the people and sent food.

Each morning the Israelites found little pieces of honey-flavored white wafers on the ground.

"What is it?" they asked. They called it manna, which means "what is it?"

Every day God sent manna. On the sixth day of the week, God sent twice as much manna, so the people wouldn't have to gather any on the seventh day. That was the day of rest.

Moses and God Speak on the Mountain

When the Israelites had traveled for three months, they made camp at the foot of a big mountain. God told Moses to tell the people He would talk to them in three days.

On the third day, a loud trumpet sounded. The mountain smoked and shook because God was on it. God gave the people the Ten Commandments or rules on how to live.

Moses climbed alone into the cloud on top of the mountain and talked to God for forty days and forty nights. God told him how His chosen people were to worship Him.

The Golden Calf

Moses was on the mountain so long, the Israelites thought he must be dead. They gave up on him and on God.

They melted all their golden jewelry together and made a golden calf. They worshiped the calf and had a great feast.

When Moses came down from the mountain, he was so angry with them, he threw down the stone tablets that had the Ten Commandments written on them. They broke into many pieces.

Moses melted the calf, crushed it into gold dust, put it in the drinking water, and made everyone drink it as part of their punishment for breaking one of God's rules.

Moses asked God to forgive the people.

The Tablets of Stone

Moses returned to the mountain again and talked to God.

Again he was gone for forty days and forty nights. But this time the people had learned their lesson, and they did not make another idol.

When Moses returned, he held another set of stone tablets in his arms. God had written the Ten Commandments upon them.

The face of Moses shined so brightly with the glory of God that he had to cover it with a thin cloth when he spoke to the people. He told the Israelites that God had forgiven them, and they believed in God again.

The Tabernacle

On the mountain, God had told Moses exactly how to build a tabernacle, a house of worship. The Israelites donated materials and built the tabernacle.

It was made like a tent, so it could be taken down and carried as the Israelites journeyed on to Canaan.

Inside the tabernacle were two rooms. Inside the smallest room, which only the priests could enter once a year, was a chest or ark. Inside the ark lay the Ten Commandments on the tablets of stone.

When the tabernacle was finished, a cloud settled over it, and it was filled with the glory of God.

Spies Go into Canaan

When the Israelites reached the border of Canaan, God told Moses to send in spies before the people marched in to capture the promised land.

Twelve men traveled through Canaan for forty days.

They returned and told about a good land with lots of food. But the cities had walls around them.

Only two spies thought they could fight the people of Canaan and win because God was with them.

The other ten spies were afraid, and the Israelites were afraid, too.

God sent them back into the desert for forty years and said only the two spies and the children would enter the promised land.

Balaam and His Donkey

In their travels, the Israelites came into the land of the Moabites. The king wanted the Israelites off his land.

He asked a wise man, Balaam, to curse them.

Balaam rode to meet the king. Three times his donkey refused to go the way Balaam wanted. Three times Balaam hit the donkey.

God gave the donkey a voice to ask why he was being punished. He had always done what Balaam had asked.

God let Balaam see the angel that had blocked the donkey's path. The angel told Balaam he could not curse the Israelites, no matter what the king said.

Moses' Last Sermon

Moses led the people back to the border of Canaan.

He knew God was not going to let him go into the promised land, so he asked God who should be the leader. God chose Joshua.

Before the Israelites crossed into the promised land, Moses reminded them of God's laws. He told them to be faithful to God, and they would have all they needed.

Moses climbed to the top of Mount Nebo and looked over the Jordan River and into the promised land where his people would live. Moses died on the mountain, and God buried him Himself.

The Jordan River Parts

The time had come for the people of Israel to cross the Jordan River into Canaan and take the land God had promised them.

The river was flooded. How could the people safely cross?

God had told Joshua to have priests lead the way, carrying the ark, which held the Ten Commandments. As soon as the priests' feet touched the water, the Jordan stopped flowing, as if held back by a dam.

The Israelites crossed the dry riverbed. Then the priests walked across. When their feet touched the shore, the Jordan River flowed again.

The Battle of Jericho

Jericho was the first city the Israelites had to capture in order to claim the land God had promised. It was inside a strong wall.

God told Joshua how to take the city.

For six days the Israelites walked once around the city wall without saying a word. Priests carried the ark, and seven more priests blew on rams' horns.

On the seventh day the Israelites walked around the wall seven times. When they heard a long blast from the priests' horns, they shouted as loud as they could.

The walls cracked and fell down.

The Lamps and Trumpets of Gideon

After many years, the Israelites began worshiping idols again, and their land was taken over. God called on a farmer named Gideon to destroy the idols and drive the Midianites off the land.

Gideon raised an army of thousands, but God told him he had too many men. He wanted only 300.

In the middle of the night, Gideon and his 300 men circled the Midianite army. Each man held a trumpet and a covered lamp. At Gideon's signal, they blew their horns and uncovered their lamps.

The Midianites thought there were thousands of soldiers and were easily defeated.

Samson Loses His Strength

Sometime later when the Philistines ruled the Israelites, God gave Samson great strength to use against his enemies. But he could never drink wine or cut his hair, or his strength would leave.

Samson fell in love with Delilah, who was a Philistine. Philistine leaders gave her money to find out where Samson got his strength.

Three times she asked, and he made up stories.

Then he told her the truth: God gave him strength through his hair that had never been cut.

While he was sleeping, Delilah had his hair cut and turned him over to his enemies.

Samson's strength was gone.

Samson's Death in the Temple

The Philistines put out both Samson's eyes and took him to prison. They made him turn a millstone to grind corn for them. They believed he couldn't hurt them anymore.

But Samson's hair began to grow. He felt stronger and stronger.

One day the Philistines held a big party in their temple. They brought Samson in so people could laugh at his weakness.

Samson stood between two stone pillars that held up the roof. He prayed to God for strength one last time.

He pushed on the pillars with all his might. The temple crashed down, killing Samson and all the Philistines inside.

Naomi and Ruth

When famine again struck Canaan, Naomi, her husband, and two sons went to Moab where there was food. Her husband died there, her sons married, and then they died too.

The famine ended, and Naomi decided to go home.

She told her daughters-in-law to go home to their families, who would take care of them.

One woman went home. The other, Ruth, decided to stay with her mother-in-law.

Naomi told Ruth they would be poor in Canaan.

But that didn't matter to Ruth.

She said, "Your people will become my people, and your God, my God."

The Love Story of Ruth and Boaz

In Canaan, Ruth and Naomi were very poor. An old law helped them find food. Workers bringing in harvest from the fields were allowed to leave some grain behind for poor people to gather.

Ruth went into the field and gathered grain behind the harvesters.

Boaz, the owner of the field, saw her and spoke to her. He told her she could drink with the harvesters and eat with them. He had the workers leave more grain behind for Ruth to harvest.

In time, Boaz and Ruth married. Naomi moved in with them and became nurse for their son.

The Good Man Job

Because Job believed in God and obeyed His laws, God blessed Job with a family and wealth.

One day God tested Job. An accident killed his children; thieves stole his oxen, donkeys, and camels. Lightning killed his sheep, and most of his servants died.

Still Job believed God knew what was best for him.

Sores broke out on Job's body, giving him constant pain.

Job asked to die, but God wouldn't let him. He complained to God, then realized he shouldn't have and asked for forgiveness.

Because Job was faithful through these bad times, God took away the sores and blessed him again.

Jonah and the Big Fish

God told the prophet Jonah to go to a wicked city and tell the people He would destroy them if they didn't change.

Since these people weren't Israelites, Jonah didn't want to go.

Instead he got on a ship and ran from God.

A great storm came up. Jonah told the sailors to throw him overboard since he had angered God, which caused the storm. Immediately the sea calmed.

Jonah sank, but a big fish swallowed him. After three days, the fish spat him out on land, and Jonah went to the city and preached.

The people believed him and worshiped the true God.

The Boy Samuel Listens to God

Because Hannah prayed for a son and told God she would give the son to Him, God answered her prayer. Samuel was born. Hannah took the young boy to the priest Eli and let him serve God.

One night Samuel heard Eli call his name, but Eli said he hadn't called him. This happened three times. Eli told Samuel that God was calling him.

The next time he heard his name, Samuel told God he was listening. God told him that Eli's sons were evil and would be punished.

Because God talked to Samuel, he later became a ruler of the Israelites.

Samuel and Saul

After Eli died, Samuel became the people's judge.

He appointed his two sons as judges, but they were not good judges.

The people wanted a king. Samuel told them they didn't need a king. God was their king. But they kept asking for a king, and God told Samuel to do as they asked.

One day a tall, handsome man came into the city.

God told Samuel that this man, Saul, would be the king. When they were alone, Samuel poured oil on Saul's head, a way of appointing him the first king of the Israelites.

King Saul led the people in many battles.

David and Goliath

The Philistines and the Israelites were at war again. The shepherd boy David delivered food to his brothers who were in Israel's army.

On the battlefield he saw Goliath, a giant twice the size of a normal man. For forty days he had challenged an Israelite to fight him.

Knowing God was with him, David stepped forward.

King Saul offered his armor, but David took his sling and some pebbles to fight the giant.

He swung his sling, and the stone hit the giant between the eyes, knocking him down. David rushed up, took the giant's sword, and killed him.

Two Special Friends

God was with David, and this made King Saul very jealous. He vowed to kill David.

Jonathan, Saul's son, was David's best friend.

David asked him to find out if he was in danger.

Later Jonathan went to a field. He shot arrows into the air ahead of a lad who was to gather them. That was the signal that David was in danger.

Jonathan sent the lad back into the city.

David came out of hiding at the edge of the field, and he and Jonathan cried, said good-bye, and said they would be with God.

David as King

David became the king of all Israel. His army fought the people of Jerusalem and won. David moved into Jerusalem, and it became known as the city of David. David's army also fought the Philistines and drove them off Israel's land.

David felt the Ark of the Covenant should be in Jerusalem, so he had it brought and put in a special tent.

But shouldn't the holy ark have a better home?

David decided to build a temple for the ark, but God told him no. He would let his son become king after him, and David's son would build the temple.

The Temple is Built

God told David he couldn't build the temple, but he could get things ready. He had stones shaped, trees cut for wood, and nails made of iron. He picked the spot where the temple would be built in Jerusalem.

While David was still alive, his son Solomon was crowned king. He started workmen building the temple, which took seven years to complete.

When it was finished, the ark with the Ten Commandments in it was moved to the inner room. Solomon prayed that God would accept the temple.

When his prayer ended, the glory of God filled the temple.

Wise King Solomon and the Baby

God gave Solomon the gift of wisdom. He was the wisest king to rule Israel.

One day two women brought a baby to his home. Both women had newborn babies, but one of the babies had died. Now both women claimed this baby.

"Bring a sword," King Solomon said. "Cut the baby in two, and each shall have a half."

"Oh, no," cried one woman. "Let the baby live."

"Cut it in half," the other woman said.

"Give the baby to the woman who wanted the baby to live," said the king. "She is the real mother."

Elijah and the Ravens

King Ahab of Israel was a very bad man. He made his people worship a false god.

This made God angry. He sent the prophet Elijah with a message. There would be no rain until King Ahab asked God to make it rain again. Without rain, crops wouldn't grow, and people would starve.

God told Elijah to hide from King Ahab in the wilderness. Elijah drank from a creek, but he had no food. Then he saw black birds flying above him. These ravens carried food in their beaks and dropped it beside Elijah. Ravens brought food each morning and night.

God had sent the ravens.

Elijah and the Widow

When the ravens could find no more food for Elijah, God sent him to the house of a widow and her little boy.

She agreed to feed Elijah, but she only had a little bit of oil and grain, enough for one loaf of bread.

Elijah said if she shared with him, she would have plenty left. She didn't run out of oil and grain. It lasted a whole year.

After this, the widow's son grew sick and died.

Could Elijah's God bring him back to life?

Elijah prayed for God to make the boy live again, and the Lord did.

The Contest

Many of the people of Israel worshiped a false god, Baal.

The Lord told Elijah to prove who was the real God.

The people were called together.

Elijah said, "I will pray to the Lord, and 450 prophets of Baal will pray to Baal. The God who sends fire is the true God."

Baal's prophets gathered wood and placed meat on top to be burned. They prayed all day. There was no fire.

Elijah gathered wood and placed meat on top. He had the people pour water on the wood and the meat. He prayed to God. Fire came from heaven.

The people cried, "The Lord is God."

Elijah Chooses Elisha

God told Elijah to choose Elisha to take his place as a prophet.

One day Elijah saw Elisha plowing in a field. He didn't say a word to him or even stop walking. As he passed by, he took off his coat and threw it over Elisha's shoulders. Elisha knew this was God's call.

"Let me kiss my father and mother, and then I will go with you," he told Elijah.

Elisha killed his oxen, roasted the meat, and gave the meat to the people on the farm as a sign he was leaving forever. He became Elijah's helper.

Elisha Cures the Leper

The king of Syria heard of Elisha and the wonderful things he did, so he sent his soldier, Naaman, for help. Naaman was sick with leprosy.

When Naaman reached Elisha's home, the prophet sent his servant out to tell Naaman to wash in the Jordan River seven times.

Naaman was angry that Elisha would send a servant to tell him something so easy.

"If it was a hard thing Elisha asked, you would do it," Naaman's servant said. "Surely you can do this simple thing."

So Naaman washed seven times in the Jordan and was cured. He then praised God's name.

The End of the Tribes

Although the Lord sent prophets like Elijah and Elisha to the Israelites, not many were led back to worship Him.

Most followed wicked kings and worshiped idol gods. So the Lord did as He promised. He let the foreigners capture the land and take the people back to their country. The ten tribes of the north were lost forever.

The two tribes in the south, Judah and Benjamin, were the people God kept separate as His chosen people. Since Judah was the largest tribe, the two tribes together were called "Judah," sometimes shortened to "Jews." Their land was called "Judea."

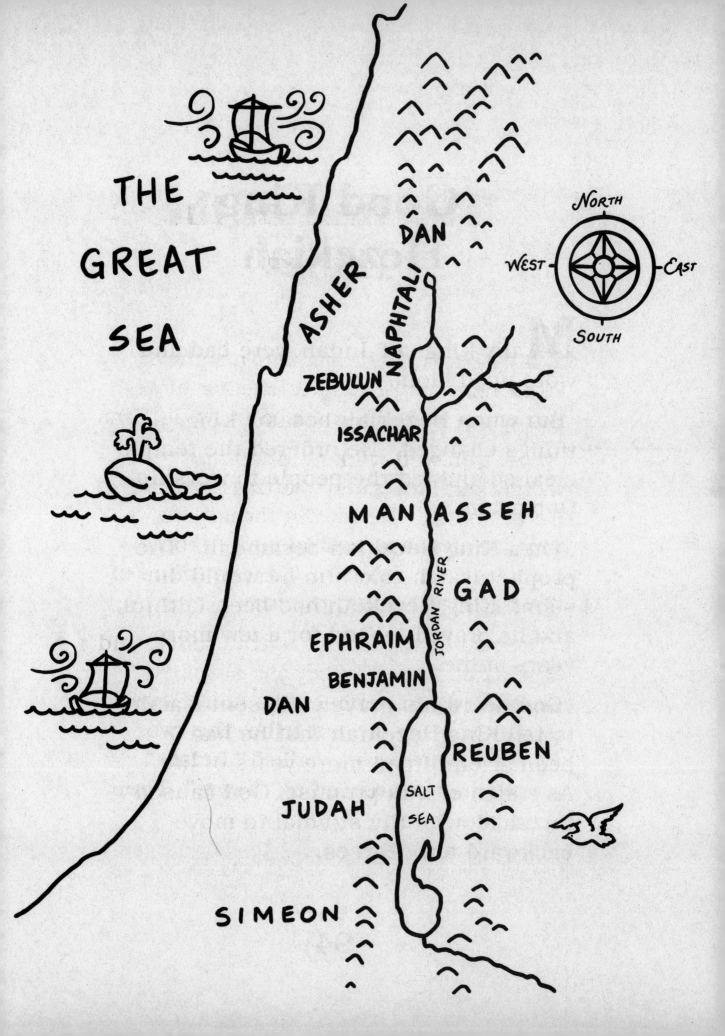

Good King Hezekiah

Many kings of Judah were bad and worshiped idols.

But when Hezekiah became king, things changed. He ordered the temple cleaned and led the people to worship God again.

Then King Hezekiah became ill. The prophet Isaiah told him he would die soon. King Hezekiah had been faithful, and he prayed to God for a few more years of life.

God heard his prayer. He sent Isaiah to tell King Hezekiah that he had been given fifteen more years of life. As a sign of this promise, God caused the shadow of the sundial to move backward ten degrees.

Daniel Interprets Nebuchadnezzar's Dream

King Nebuchadnezzar had many wise men. Among them was Daniel, a Jew.

One night the king had a terrible dream, but he could not remember it in the morning. He asked some of his wise men to tell him the dream and its meaning.

No one could.

The king ordered all the wise men killed.

Daniel was taken prisoner with the rest of the wise men. However, he prayed to God, and God explained the dream.

Daniel was taken before the king and told him what the dream was and what it meant.

The king made Daniel a leader and gave him many gifts.

The Fiery Furnace

King Nebuchadnezzar made a gold statue ninety feet high. He commanded all his subjects to bow down to this god, or they would be burned to death.

Three Jews—Shadrach, Meshach, and Abednego—refused to bow down to any god but the true God.

They were tied, taken to the fiery furnace, and pushed in.

The king looked inside the furnace and saw four men walking around.

How could this be?

God had sent an angel to protect the men.

When the king called the men out of the fire, their clothes weren't burnt, and they didn't smell like smoke.

The Handwriting on the Wall

King Belshazzar of Babylon had a great feast in a temple. He took the golden cups that had been in God's Temple in Jerusalem and let his princes drink from them.

This made God angry. He sent a hand to write on the wall of the temple.

The king asked that the wise man Daniel tell him what the strange words meant.

Daniel said the king's empire was coming to an end.

His kingdom would be divided and given to a foreign power.

That night, the Medes and the Persians captured the city and killed the king.

Daniel in the Lion's Den

When the Persians took over the city, Daniel was made a leader. Other leaders were jealous of him. They asked the king to pass a law saying for thirty days no one could pray to any god or man except the king, or he'd be killed.

King Darius signed the law.

The other leaders saw Daniel praying to God. They told the king, and Daniel was thrown into a den of hungry lions.

"Your God will protect you," King Darius said.

The next morning Daniel, unharmed, walked out of the den. God had sent an angel to shut the mouths of the lions.

Rebuilding Jerusalem

Seventy years after the Jews had been taken to Babylon, King Cyrus sent out word that anyone from Judah who wanted to go to Jerusalem and rebuild the temple was free to go.

Just as Jeremiah the prophet had told the Jews, after seventy years they could return to the promised land.

The first thing the Jews built was an altar. Then they started on the temple. A new Persian king stopped the building, but the next king let them finish the temple.

It took twenty years to rebuild, but at last God's temple was completed.

Queen Esther Saves Her People

Not all the Jews returned to Canaan from Persia.

Esther stayed, and King Ahasuerus selected her as his queen.

The king had an evil advisor named Haman. He made a law that on a certain day anyone could kill a Jew and take his land.

When Esther heard about it, she talked to the king.

The law could not be changed, but the king had Haman killed.

Then he passed a new law that on the day the Jews were to be killed, they could fight off anyone who attacked them. They did this and defeated everyone who fought them.

Building the Wall

In Persia, Nehemiah served the king as cup bearer.

He heard that Jerusalem did not have a wall around it for protection. This made him frown.

"Why are you sad?" the king asked.

Nehemiah told him, and the king said he could go to Jerusalem and build the wall.

The people of Jerusalem were glad to work with Nehemiah.

Enemies of the Jews didn't want the wall built. So Nehemiah divided the workmen in two. While half of them built the wall, the other half stood guard.

The people worked day and night, and the wall was finished in fifty-two days.

An Angel Visits Mary

God sent the angel Gabriel to a village in Galilee, which was ruled by the Romans.

Gabriel appeared to a young girl named Mary and said, "The Lord is with you!"

Mary didn't know what that meant.

"Don't be frightened," the angel said. He told her that she had been chosen to have a baby boy, who would be the Son of God. He would be the Savior whom God had promised to His people.

The angel told her the Holy Spirit would come upon her, and she would have God's Son. And she should name him Jesus.

Jesus is Born
in the Stable

When Mary was due to have her baby, she traveled with Joseph to the city of Bethlehem. The Romans had ordered everyone to go to the city where their families had lived and be counted on tax lists.

The roads were full with travelers going to be counted. They rented every room they could find.

When Mary and Joseph got to Bethlehem, there were no rooms left. They spent the night in the stable of an inn.

And that is where Jesus was born.

Mary wrapped Him up and placed Him in a bed of hay in a manger.

The Shepherds

In the fields were shepherds, watching their sheep through the night.

An angel came to them, and the glory of the Lord shone around the shepherds, scaring them.

The angel said, "Don't be afraid. For I bring you great news. The Savior is born in Bethlehem. You'll find Him lying in a manger."

And suddenly there were many angels' voices praising God and saying, "Glory to God in the highest, and on earth peace, good will toward men."

The shepherds hurried to Bethlehem. They found the stable and the baby Jesus.

The Wise Men

Three wise men from the East saw a new star in the sky and knew it was a special sign.

They traveled to Jerusalem and asked about the child who would be king of the Jews. King Herod heard about them and asked them to return to him if they found the child. He wanted to kill the baby, so he would still be king.

The star appeared again and guided the wise men to Bethlehem, where they found the baby Jesus. They gave Him gifts of gold, frankincense, and myrrh. They didn't tell the king they'd found the baby.

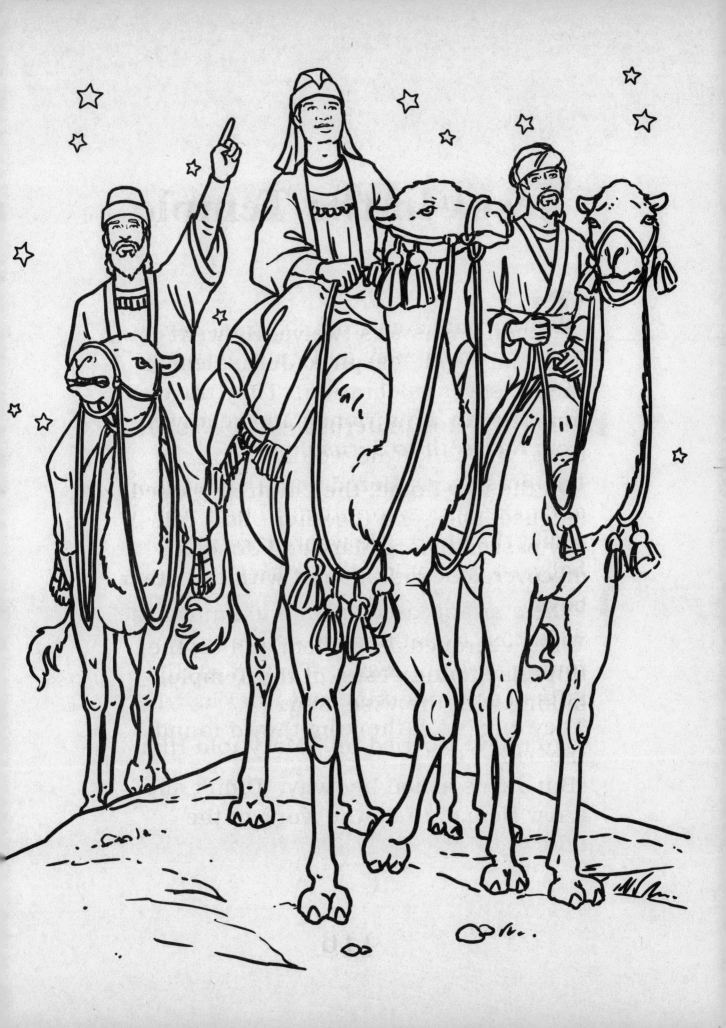

Jesus in the Temple

When Jesus was twelve, He went with Mary and Joseph to Jerusalem for the Passover celebration. They traveled in a caravan with friends and relatives from Nazareth to Jerusalem.

On the way home, the children walked, laughed, and sang together. So a full day passed before Mary and Joseph discovered Jesus was not with the other boys.

They searched Jerusalem and on the third day found Jesus in the Temple, talking with the wise men.

"You have worried us," Mary told Him.

But Jesus asked her why. Didn't she know He had to do the work of the Lord?

John the Baptist

John was born a few months before Jesus. He knew he had been chosen to get the people ready to meet Jesus.

He lived in the wilderness for many years, praying to God and thinking about the Savior.

Then God called him to leave the wilderness and go to the land near the Jordan River.

John told the people to turn from doing wrong and be baptized to show that their hearts were clean. Then they would be ready for the Kingdom of Heaven, which would come soon.

He baptized many people and earned the name John the Baptist.

The Baptism of Jesus

One day Jesus came to the Jordan River and asked John to baptize Him. God had told John that Jesus was the Savior.

How could he baptize the Savior?

"I am the one who should be baptized by you," John said.

But Jesus told him it was the right thing to do, and John agreed.

As Jesus came out of the waters of the Jordan River, the Holy Spirit, in the form of a dove, lit on Him.

Then God spoke from heaven and said, "This is my beloved Son, with whom I am very pleased."

Forty Days in the Wilderness

After He was baptized, Jesus spent the next forty days in the wilderness, praying and eating nothing.

He was tested three times by the devil.

Jesus was hungry, and the devil said, "Change these stones into bread."

But Jesus said, "No." He would obey God.

Next the devil told Him to jump off the roof of the temple, and the angels would save Him.

But Jesus said, "No."

The devil took Him to the top of a mountain and showed Him riches. "Worship me, and all this is Yours."

Jesus said, "No." He would worship only God.

Jesus Teaches the People

Wherever Jesus went, crowds of people gathered to hear Him speak. They also came to see Him heal the sick.

Jesus traveled throughout the land, teaching in synagogues and preaching the good news to the people.

What was the good news? Jesus came to be punished for our sins. If we believe in Him and are sorry for our sins, we will not be punished when we die, but will go to heaven and live there forever.

There were religious leaders who did not believe Jesus was the Son of God. But many people loved Jesus and followed Him everywhere.

Water to Wine

One day Jesus and some followers went to His home and found that His mother, Mary, was going to a wedding.

"Come with me," Mary said. "You will be welcomed."

The guests at the wedding celebrated with a dinner party and had fun with their friends.

After a while Mary came to Jesus and said, "They have run out of wine."

Jesus asked the servants to fill six water jugs with water.

"Now," he said, "take some to the ruler of the feast."

The servants dipped into a water jug and found not water, but a delicious wine.

Fishers of Men

Jesus was busy healing the sick. So many people asked for His help, that He had little time to teach the Word of God.

He needed helpers.

To the fishermen Simon Peter and his brother, Andrew, He said, "Put down your nets and follow me. I will make you fishers of men." That meant that they would fish for the souls of men by leading them to the Lord.

He granted the power to heal and the ability to preach to twelve men. These apostles were: Simon Peter, Andrew, James, John, Philip, Bartholomew, Thomas, Matthew, James, Judas, Simon, and Judas Iscariot.

The Woman at the Well

While traveling through Samaria, Jesus grew tired and sat beside a well while His disciples went to buy food.

A woman came to the well.

Jesus asked for a drink.

"A Jew asking a Samaritan for water?" she asked.

Usually Jews wouldn't even speak to Samaritans.

Jesus told her that He could grant her "living water" that was the Spirit of His love. He explained that He was the Savior and told her things about herself that He couldn't know.

She believed Him and told others in the town about Him.

Jesus stayed there for two days teaching the Samaritans.

A Mustard Seed

Jesus taught his followers about God's love by using parables or stories that have a special meaning.

One of His parables was about a mustard seed. It is a tiny, tiny seed. But when it is planted and taken care of, the little seed grows into a bush big enough for birds to build their nests in it.

Jesus said it was the same with our love for God.

At first it seems very small, but it will grow stronger and stronger every day, if we love God and try to please Him.

Calming the Waters

One evening Jesus and His apostles got into a boat and began to cross the Sea of Galilee. Jesus was tired and fell asleep.

On the way, a storm came up. The sky grew black with clouds, and the wind blew hard. The waves grew bigger and bigger, splashing into the boat and filling it with water.

After bailing out what water they could, the apostles grew afraid.

"Wake up and save us," they cried to Jesus.

Jesus awoke and told the water to be still.

Immediately the sea was calm.

"Why were you afraid? I'm with you," He said.

Bringing Jairus's Daughter to Life

Jairus, the ruler of a synagogue, heard that Jesus was coming to his town. Jairus' daughter was very ill, near death, and he wanted Jesus to heal her.

He made his way through the crowd and talked to Jesus.

They walked back to his house. Before they reached it, a messenger told them that the girl was dead.

Jesus told Jairus to believe in Him, and his daughter would be made well.

Jesus went into the girl's room and held her hand.

"Get up," He said.

The girl stood up and walked to her mother and father.

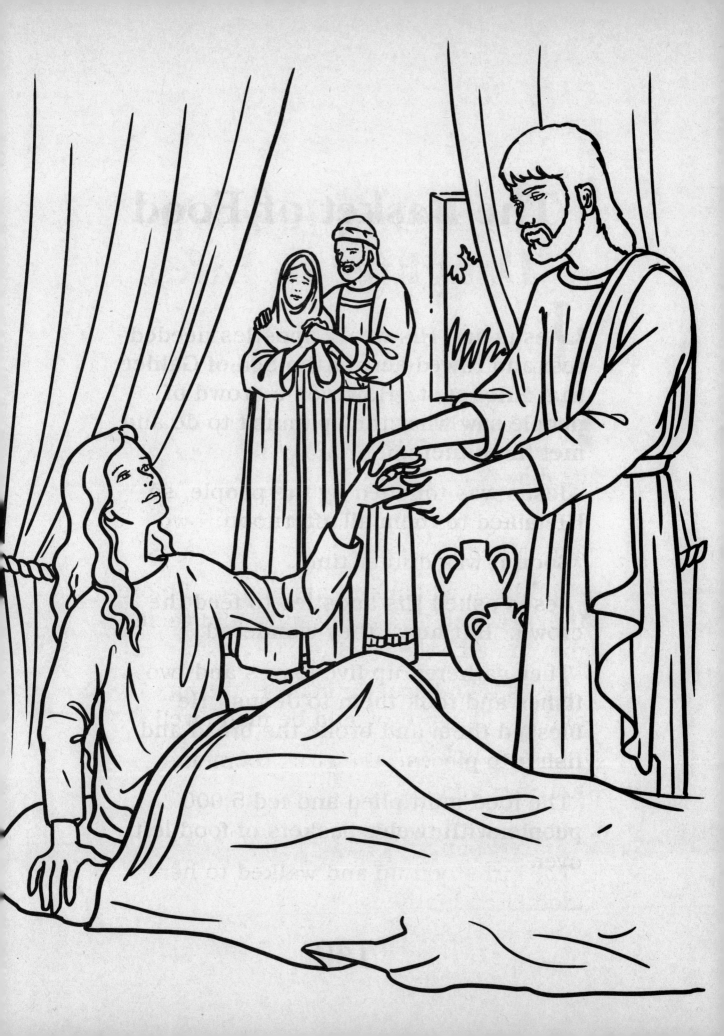

The Basket of Food

Jesus and His weary apostles needed rest and rowed across the Sea of Galilee to a quiet spot. However, a crowd of people saw what they planned to do and met them there.

Jesus was touched by the people, so He talked to them all afternoon.

Soon it was dinner time.

Jesus asked His apostles to feed the crowd. But how? they wondered.

They gathered up five loaves and two fishes and took them to Jesus. He blessed them and broke the bread and fish into pieces.

The food multiplied and fed 5,000 people, with twelve baskets of food left over.

Walking on Water

Jesus ordered His apostles to sail without Him. He climbed a mountain to pray, and He could see His apostles were in trouble on a stormy sea.

Jesus walked toward the boat on top of the water, as if it was land.

The apostles were afraid until Jesus told them who He was.

"May I walk to you?" Peter asked.

"Yes, Peter."

Peter walked on top of the water, until he looked down in the waves and was scared. He started sinking.

Jesus saved him and told him he should have more faith.

The apostles said, "Truly you are the Son of God."

Glory on the Mountain

Jesus had told His disciples that He would be killed by the Jews in Jerusalem and would rise three days later, but they didn't understand.

One day Jesus took his apostles Peter, James, and John to the top of a mountain to pray.

Suddenly Jesus' face became very bright, as bright as the sun. Then two men appeared beside Him. Moses and Elijah had come to talk to Jesus about being killed in Jerusalem.

A cloud covered the mountain and the apostles heard the voice of God say, "This is My beloved son. Listen to Him."

The Blind Man Healed

One day as Jesus was walking along, He saw a man who had been born blind. The man had never seen his parents or friends.

To demonstrate the power of God, Jesus spat on the ground, made mud, and smoothed it over the blind man's eyes.

"Go and wash in the Pool of Siloam," He said.

So the man went where he was sent, washed, and came back seeing.

Others asked him who the man was who had healed him.

"I don't know whether He is good or bad," the man said, "but I know this: I was blind, and now I see."

Lazarus Arises from the Dead

Mary, Martha, and their brother, Lazarus, loved Jesus.

When Lazarus got sick, his sisters sent a messenger to Jesus to ask Him to come heal their brother.

But Jesus did not arrive in time. Lazarus had been dead for four days.

"If only you had been here, my brother would be alive," Martha said.

Jesus and a crowd went to the cave where Lazarus was buried. He ordered men to take the stone away that blocked the cave, and they did.

"Lazarus, come out!" Jesus said.

And Lazarus walked out, alive.

Some said, "Jesus is the Son of God!"

The Son Who Came Back Home

A man had two sons. One son asked for his share of the family money. Then he left home.

He did many bad things. He spent all his money, and he was hungry. He knew even his father's servants had good food, so he went home.

"I am sorry, father," he said. He asked for a job as a servant. The father was happy his son had come back. He made a big dinner for him.

The other son was angry. He had always done right.

Why treat his brother so well?

"All I have is yours," the father said. "But it is right to celebrate your brother's return."

The Good Samaritan

One day a man was walking alone on the road. Some bandits robbed him and beat him up. He was bleeding and needed help.

A priest came by, looked at the man, but kept right on going.

A Jewish temple assistant walked by the man. He looked at him, but walked on.

A man from Samaria, a country many people hated, traveled on the road. He saw the man and stopped. He bandaged him, took him to an inn, and paid the innkeeper to take care of him.

This Samaritan obeyed the golden rule: Treat others as you want to be treated.

The Little Children

It was wonderful to be near Jesus. Men and women came to hear him. Sometimes mothers brought their children, who would sit at Jesus' feet.

The mothers asked Jesus to bless their children.

The apostles told the mothers to keep the children away. Jesus was too busy to be bothered by them.

Jesus told the apostles they were wrong.

"Let the little children come to me," He said. He held the children and looked up to heaven and prayed. He blessed them.

He said the Kingdom of God belonged to men who had hearts as trusting as children.

A Little Man
in a Tree

Zacchaeus, a rich man, made his fortune by cheating others. One day Zacchaeus, who was very short, heard that Jesus was coming to his town. He wanted to see Him and waited for Him to come.

But the crowd blocked Jesus from Zacchaeus' view.

He climbed a sycamore tree and looked down.

Jesus looked up and said, "Zacchaeus, come down out of that tree. I must go to your house today."

Zacchaeus smiled and changed his ways. "I will give half my money to the poor. And if I cheated someone, I'll pay him back four times the money."

Jesus Rides into the City

Jesus walked along the road to Jerusalem. Many other people walked with Him.

Jesus asked two of His disciples to go into a village.

There they would find a little donkey tied. They were to bring the donkey to Jesus.

The men brought the donkey to Jesus. They put their coats on it to make a saddle.

Jesus sat on the little donkey. People put their coats on the road to make a carpet for Jesus to ride on. Others cut branches off trees to make a carpet of leaves.

The people sang "Hosanna!" They were happy Jesus had come.

Mary's Gift

Mary loved Jesus very much. She wanted to give Him something special. The best thing she had was a jar of wonderful smelling perfumed oil.

She went to the house where Jesus was eating dinner. She poured the oil on His head. She poured the oil on His feet and dried them with her hair.

One of the men with Jesus was angry. This oil could have been sold for money. The money could have been given to the poor.

But Jesus told the men that the poor always would be with them, but that He would not.

Mary's gift was a gift of love.

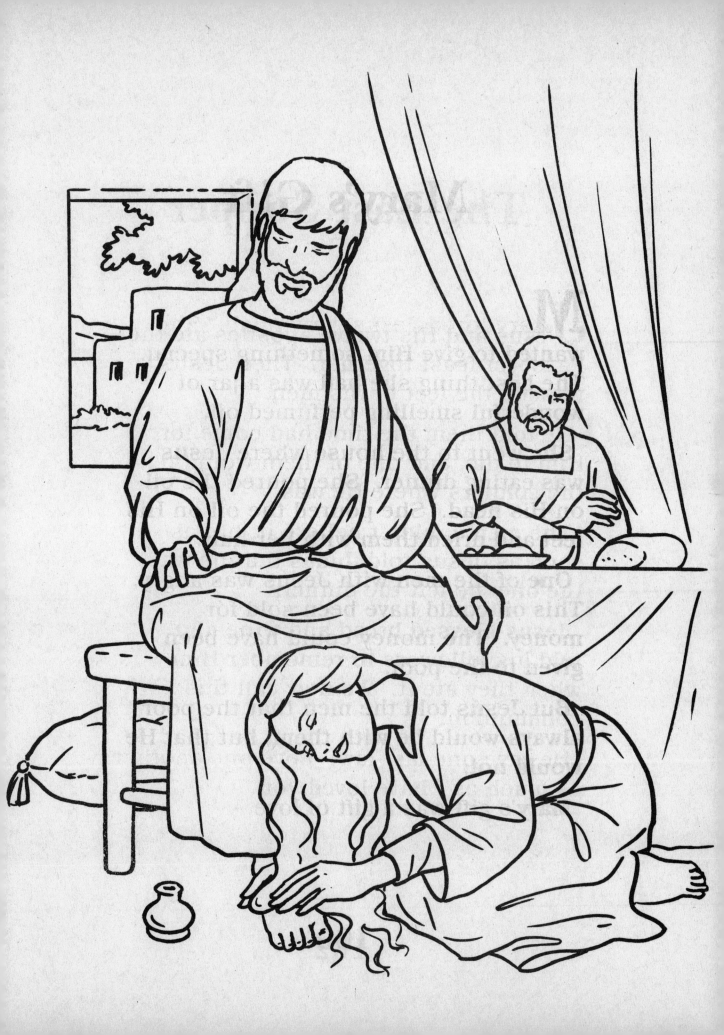

The Last Supper

Jesus and His twelve apostles ate the Passover feast together. Then Jesus washed the feet of His men.

He told them the time had come for Him to die, and one of them would tell the soldiers where He was.

The men couldn't believe it, but as soon as Jesus told Judas that he was the one, he left the dinner.

Jesus blessed bread and wine and told his followers to remember Him when they ate it. We now call this communion.

He gave one last law: Love one another as much as I have loved you.

Jesus Prays
in the Garden

After the Passover feast, Jesus and His eleven apostles walked to a garden on the Mount of Olives. Jesus asked His men to keep their eyes open and watch for trouble while He prayed.

He walked on alone and fell to the ground and prayed to His Heavenly Father. Jesus knew He was going to die, and He knew He would suffer terribly.

He told God how He felt, but said He would follow God's orders. He prayed three times, and the final time an angel came from above and comforted Him and gave Him strength to face His death.

A Kiss from Judas

While Jesus and His eleven apostles prayed in the garden, Judas sought the temple priests who didn't believe Jesus was the Son of God. He told them now was the time for their soldiers to capture Jesus. Judas would show them which one He was by kissing Jesus.

Judas led a mob back to the garden. He kissed Jesus on the cheek.

Jesus told His disciples not to fight the soldiers.

He could call thousands of angels if He wanted, but it was time for Him to die for the people.

The soldiers arrested Jesus for claiming to be the Son of God.

Peter Denies Jesus

Jesus had told Peter that he would deny knowing Him three times before the rooster crowed, but Peter didn't believe Him. He loved Jesus.

As the soldiers took Jesus away, Peter followed them. He watched them spit on and hit Jesus, and he was scared.

A girl asked if he were with Jesus.

"I don't know what you're talking about," Peter said.

On the porch another girl asked if he were with Jesus.

"I don't know the man," Peter said.

Some men asked him about Jesus.

"I don't know Him."

Then the rooster crowed. And Peter cried.

The Verdict

Although the Jewish priests wanted to kill Jesus for claiming to be the Son of God, they couldn't without permission of the Roman governor, Pontius Pilate. The Roman governor saw no reason to kill Jesus.

Each year a Jewish prisoner was released from prison as part of the Passover celebration. Pilate said Jesus could be the prisoner. But the priests wanted Jesus killed, and they convinced the people to choose to release a murderer instead.

"Crucify Jesus," the crowd yelled.

Pilate gave permission, but said, "I am not to blame for the death of this innocent man."

Jesus is Crucified

Friday morning Jesus was taken to a hill called "Calvary." There He was nailed onto a cross, and the cross was stuck into the ground. People who were crucified didn't die right away.

They lived for hours in terrible pain.

At noon, darkness fell all over the land and lasted three hours. At the end of that time, Jesus said, "It is finished," and died.

The earth shook, rocks shattered, and the curtain in the temple was ripped in half by unseen hands.

The Roman soldiers were afraid, and one said, "Surely, this man was the Son of God."

The Resurrection

Jesus' body was taken to a tomb, and a rock was rolled into the entrance to block it. Roman soldiers guarded the tomb.

There was no time to anoint the body before the Sabbath began. Early Sunday morning three women went to the tomb to anoint the body. They found the rock rolled away and the tomb empty.

An angel stood guard. "Do not be afraid. Jesus is not here. He has risen from the dead," he told them.

The women rushed to tell the disciples and met Jesus on the way.

He told them to have the disciples meet Him in Galilee.

Jesus Appears to His Apostles

Jesus met his apostles in Galilee and during the next forty days, He appeared to them many times. He asked them to go out and preach to the people of the world. Although He could not go with them, He would send the Holy Spirit to help with their work.

At the end of forty days, as Jesus was blessing them, the disciples saw Him rise into heaven.

Two angels spoke to them.

"This same Jesus you saw taken up into heaven will come down again in the clouds, just as you saw Him go up."

The Holy Spirit Comes

As Jesus had told them to do, His apostles and disciples waited in Jerusalem for the Holy Spirit to come to them.

On the day of the harvest celebration, called Pentecost, about 120 disciples had gathered together. Suddenly the sound of wind filled the house they were in. What looked like flames of fire came down, and one rested on the head of each person.

The Holy Spirit filled each of them.

The Holy Spirit gave the disciples the ability to speak languages they didn't know. People from other countries could understand them because the disciples spoke about the wonderful works of God in their own language.

Peter and John and the Beggar

As Peter and John went to the temple one afternoon, they saw a crippled man being carried to the temple gate, where he begged every day.

He asked them for some money.

"Look here," Peter said.

The crippled man looked up, expecting money.

"We don't have any money for you," said Peter, "but I'll give you something else. I command you in the name of Jesus Christ of Nazareth, walk!"

Peter helped the crippled man to his feet. The man took one step, then another. Soon he was leaping for joy.

Faith in Jesus had let him walk again.

Philip and the Egyptian

An angel of the Lord appeared to Philip and told him to go to a certain road about noon.

So Philip went. He saw a government official of an African country riding in a chariot. The man was reading Scripture.

Philip ran beside the chariot. "Do you know what you're reading?"

"No," said the man. He asked Philip to explain it to him.

Philip told him all about Jesus.

When they came to a pool of water, the African asked to be baptized.

"If you believe."

"I believe Jesus Christ is the Son of God."

Philip baptized him.

The Conversion of Saul

Saul was a wicked man who wanted to kill all the people who believed in Jesus.

He got permission to travel to Damascus to find believers and to bring them to Jerusalem in chains.

On the way, a bright spotlight from heaven shone on him, blinding him.

A voice said, "Saul, Saul! Why are you persecuting me?"

"Who is it?"

"I'm Jesus. Go into the city and wait for my instructions."

Saul's men led him into the city, where he didn't eat or drink for three days.

The Lord sent a disciple to Saul, who baptized him and cured his blindness.

The Gentiles

Up to this time, all the followers of Jesus were Jewish.

But non-Jews were interested in Jesus, too. They were called Gentiles.

An angel appeared to a Roman soldier and told him to speak to the apostle Peter.

At the same time, Peter had a vision. He saw all types of animals, some that Moses had said were unclean.

A voice said, "What God has made clean you cannot call unclean."

When the Roman soldier came to him, Peter understood the vision. God wanted all men, not just Jews, to be baptized with the Holy Spirit.

An Angel Rescues Peter

King Herod arrested the apostle Peter and planned to kill him after the Passover celebration. Sixteen soldiers guarded Peter in prison.

The night before he was to be killed, he was asleep, chained between two soldiers.

An angel woke him up, and the chains fell off his wrists.

"Get dressed, and put on your shoes," the angel said.

And he did.

"Put on your coat and follow me."

Peter followed the angel, but he thought he was dreaming.

Out on the street, the angel disappeared, and Peter was left alone.

Now he knew God had sent the angel to save him.

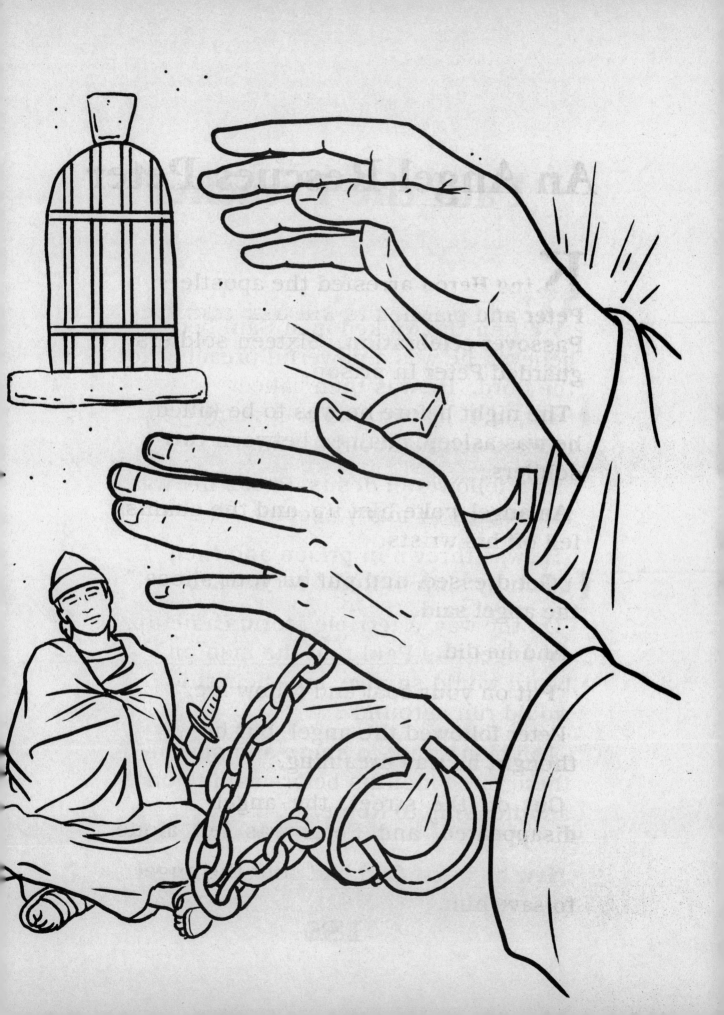

Paul the Preacher

When the wicked man Saul became a believer, he was a powerful preacher for the Lord. He was then called Paul, and he traveled over many lands teaching about Jesus.

As a follower of Jesus, Paul's life was threatened by many people.

He was thrown in prison and then taken by ship to Rome for a trial.

On the way, a terrible storm came up. An angel told Paul that the men on board would survive, but their ship would run aground.

The men swam to shore and stayed there three months before sailing on another ship to Rome.

Published by Barbour & Company, Inc.
P.O. Box 719
Uhrichsville, Ohio 44683
e-mail: books<barbour@tusco.net>

 Member of the
Evangelical Christian
Publishers Association

Printed in the United States of America